dino doodling
This journal belongs to
....

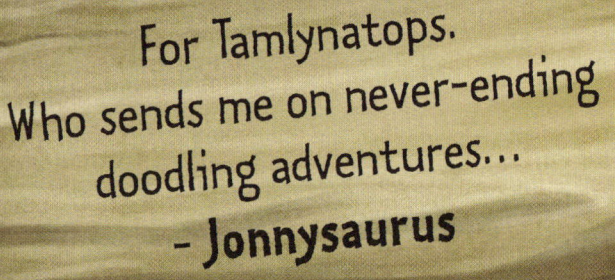

For Tamlynatops,
Who sends me on never-ending
doodling adventures...
- Jonnysaurus

A TEMPLAR BOOK

First published in the UK in 2024 by Templar Books,
an imprint of Bonnier Books UK,
4th Floor, Victoria House,
Bloomsbury Square, London WC1B 4DA
Owned by Bonnier Books
Sveavägen 56, Stockholm, Sweden
www.bonnierbooks.co.uk

Text copyright © 2024 by Jonny Duddle
Illustration copyright © 2024 by Jonny Duddle
Design copyright © 2024 by Templar Books

1 3 5 7 9 10 8 6 4 2

All rights reserved

ISBN 978-1-80078-437-6

This book was typeset in Kosmik and Zemke Hand
The illustrations were created with digital mediums and coloured pencils

Additonal text by Camilla de la Bedoyere
Edited by Rachael Roberts
Designed by Laura Hall
Production by Neil Randles

Printed in Latvia

Doodle with Duddle
How to Draw DINOSAURS

JONNY DUDDLE

templar books

HELLO BUDDING DINO-DOODLERS!

My name is Jonny Duddle and I've been doodling since I could hold a pencil. I doodled at school, I doodled at university, and now that I'm a grown-up, doodling is my job. I spend all day doodling at home and writing books, and one of my favourite things to doodle is dinosaurs. I even wrote a prehistoric book called *Gigantosaurus*. If you've picked up *How to Draw Dinosaurs*, you must like doodling dinosaurs too.

Luckily for you, this is my dino-doodling journal, and I'm going to take you on an adventure. I'll teach you how to draw these amazing creatures, and sprinkle some fascinating facts along the way.

Drawing can be tricky (I still find it hard sometimes), but by the end of this book, you'll be a much more confident dino-doodler. Before embarking on a doodling adventure, I like to be prepared. Check out the stuff I take with me and LET'S DOODLE!

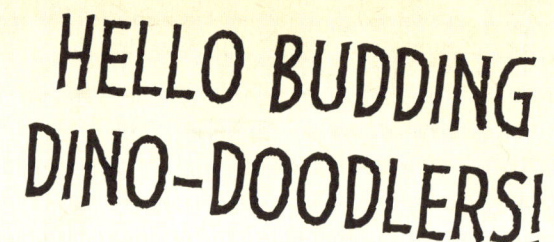

Pith helmet
For keeping the hot Welsh sun off my shiny head.

Bag
For pencils, sketchbooks, fossils and chocolate.

Pencil
For doodling dinosaurs.

Sketchbook
For doodling and writing stuff down before I forget.

Knobbly knees
Maybe you don't need these...

You don't need expensive equipment or art materials to be an artist, you just need a pencil to start. Every artist doodles with something different. I've tried everything over the years, but here are a few of my favourites:

Pencils
Any pencil will do. I like soft pencils that make dark lines. You might want an eraser to rub out lines that go wrong.

Coloured pencils
I doodle with coloured pencils a lot (look at my sketchbook pages here). You could try coloured pencils, or crayons or chalk.

Pens
Felt tips, ink pens and biros are all good for drawing, but you need to be confident as you can't rub them out!

Paints
I like watercolours because you can take them anywhere. Just add water to mix millions of colours.

Sketchbooks
My drawings are messy and rarely go right first time!

INTRODUCING THE DINOSAURS

To get started, I'd like to introduce you to some of my favourite dinosaurs. In the story I wrote, there were four little dinosaurs on the trail of the fearsome Gigantosaurus. You'll learn how to doodle them all – including Giganto – on this dino-doodling journey!

But how did these characters come to life, I hear you ask? Well, the story of *Gigantosaurus* started in my sketchbook. Sketchbooks are brilliant for drawing things you see on your travels, and writing down ideas. Years ago, I visited the Natural History Museum in London and sketched some dinosaur skeletons, which inspired me to write a tale.

While doodling characters, I wrote a list of all my favourite dinosaurs. I was a bit annoyed when I realised the four I had picked didn't exist at the same time. I carried on and hoped nobody would mind, but have a look at the timeline below to see just how far apart they existed in real life!

Have you read the *Gigantosaurus* book? Or maybe you have seen it on TV, in which case, you might know the characters by slightly different names. Maybe you've never heard of them at all! Here are some handy introductions...

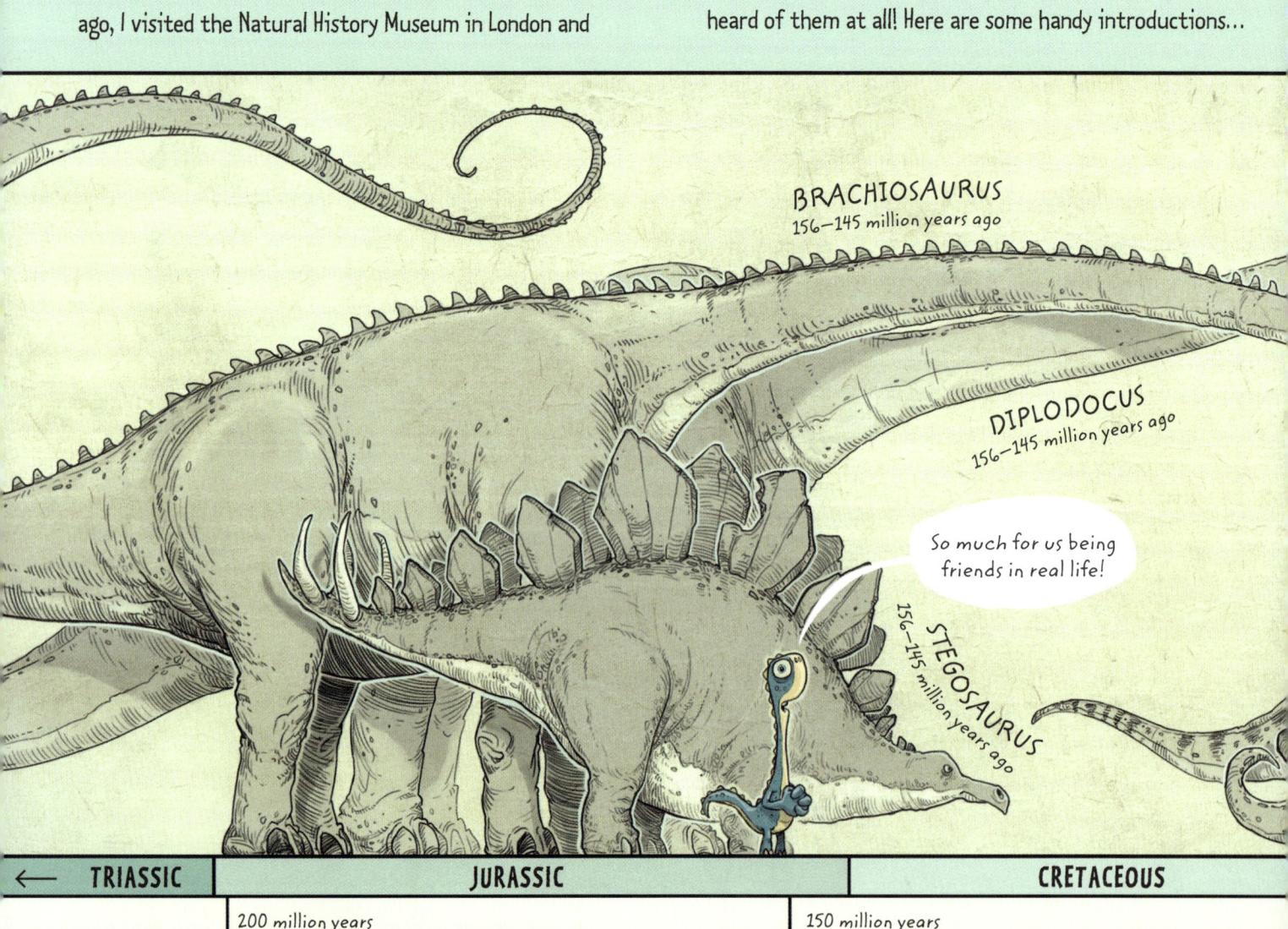

BRACHIOSAURUS
156–145 million years ago

DIPLODOCUS
156–145 million years ago

STEGOSAURUS
156–145 million years ago

So much for us being friends in real life!

← TRIASSIC	JURASSIC	CRETACEOUS
	200 million years	150 million years

DOODLE A... TRICERATOPS

Triceratops was like an oversized rhinoceros, but with extra horns and a huge heaving tail. It could grow up to nine metres long – that's longer than two cars! Palaeontologists have found more Triceratops fossils than any other dinosaur, so we know a LOT about them.

Triceratops' bony frill could be as wide as two metres – that's wider than me lying down, even wearing my big hat!

Triceratops' horns were covered by a material called keratin – you have some in your fingernails, but hopefully you trim them so they're less long and pointy.

The 'tri' in Triceratops means three. Think tricycle, triangle or tripod. Triceratops had three horns.

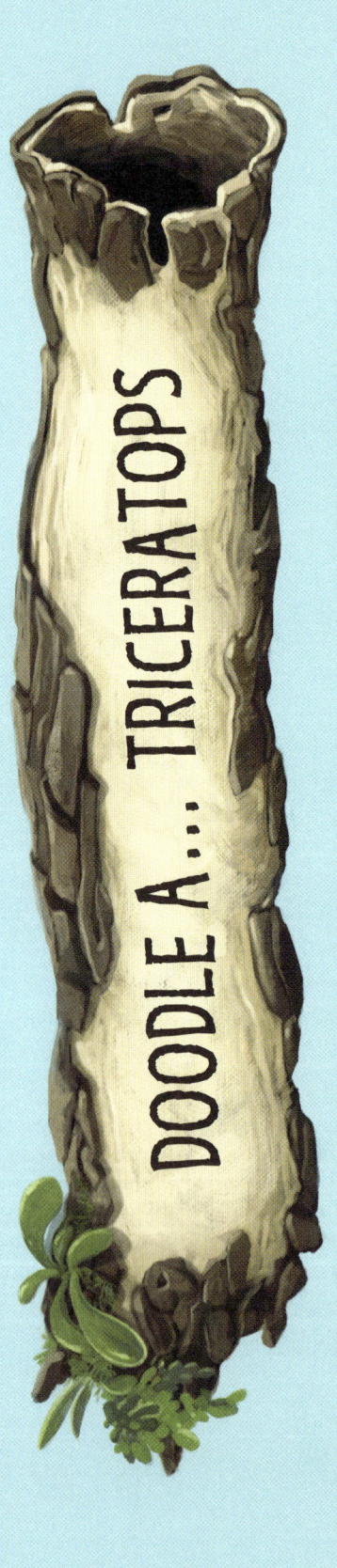

1

The shape of a Triceratops is like an egg, with a tail and a pointy head. Try drawing it lightly first. When you press harder to make a darker line, leave gaps on the underside for the legs.

2

Add four chunky legs, three horns, a small circle for the eye and a pointed beak. Draw a bumpy frill that joins to Triceratops' curvy mouth. Add a nostril too!

3

Draw in details: wrinkles where the legs join the body, bumps along its back, scales and shading on the far-side legs and horn.

Use this faint drawing to practise a Triceratops, and perhaps draw a bigger one on a piece of paper.

What colour would your Triceratops be? Would it have patterns on its body or its bony frill?

HOW TO DOODLE... FIN

Fin is a Triceratops who is a little bit shy. Have a go at doodling her using this step-by-step guide!

1 Draw Fin's beak first: three curved lines with a tiny crease where the mouth meets her face.

2 Draw a line for the bottom beak. Add a round eye either side and two black pupils, leaving a dot of white.

3 Draw the frill around Fin's head. It can be wavy, or just round. Add two stumpy horns just above her eyes.

4 Next, lightly draw the body like a teardrop. Leave gaps for the tail and the near-side leg and arm.

5 Doodle a curved tail and two legs. The leg in front extends into the body a bit, the other goes behind.

6 Draw Fin's arms and the bendy thumb on the right hand, plus three round fingers. The left hand is like three small sausages hanging from the arm.

7 Add bumps around the frill and along Fin's back and tail. Draw a line along her body where her colour is different.

8 Doodle more details: creases on her knees and around her eyes and horns. Draw a circle around each pupil.

9 For the bow, draw two curved bits of wood, with strings going from the hand to the tips, and an arrow.

You can add colour to your drawing if you like. Fin is green, with a tan belly and bony bits, a grey beak and green eyes.

Try drawing Fin on top of this faint doodle before doodling her from scratch in the space below!

FASCINATING FOSSILS

How do we know so much about dinosaurs? We learn from fossils – the ancient remains of an animal or plant that have turned to stone over millions of years. Fossils can range in size from tiny shells to an enormous Triceratops skull.

Fossils come in all shapes and sizes, and they aren't all just bones either...

Pieces of fossilised dinosaur poo are called coprolites.

What do you think this fossil could be? Try drawing the dinosaur over the top!

How Fossils Form

Imagine a Diplodocus has died, its body lying beside a river. The skin and muscle slowly rots away, leaving just the bones and teeth. Over time, the river covers the skeleton in mud and silt.

Many more layers of mud build up on top of the Diplodocus' skeleton. This squashes the layers of earth below and eventually, over thousands of years, the earth turns into rock.

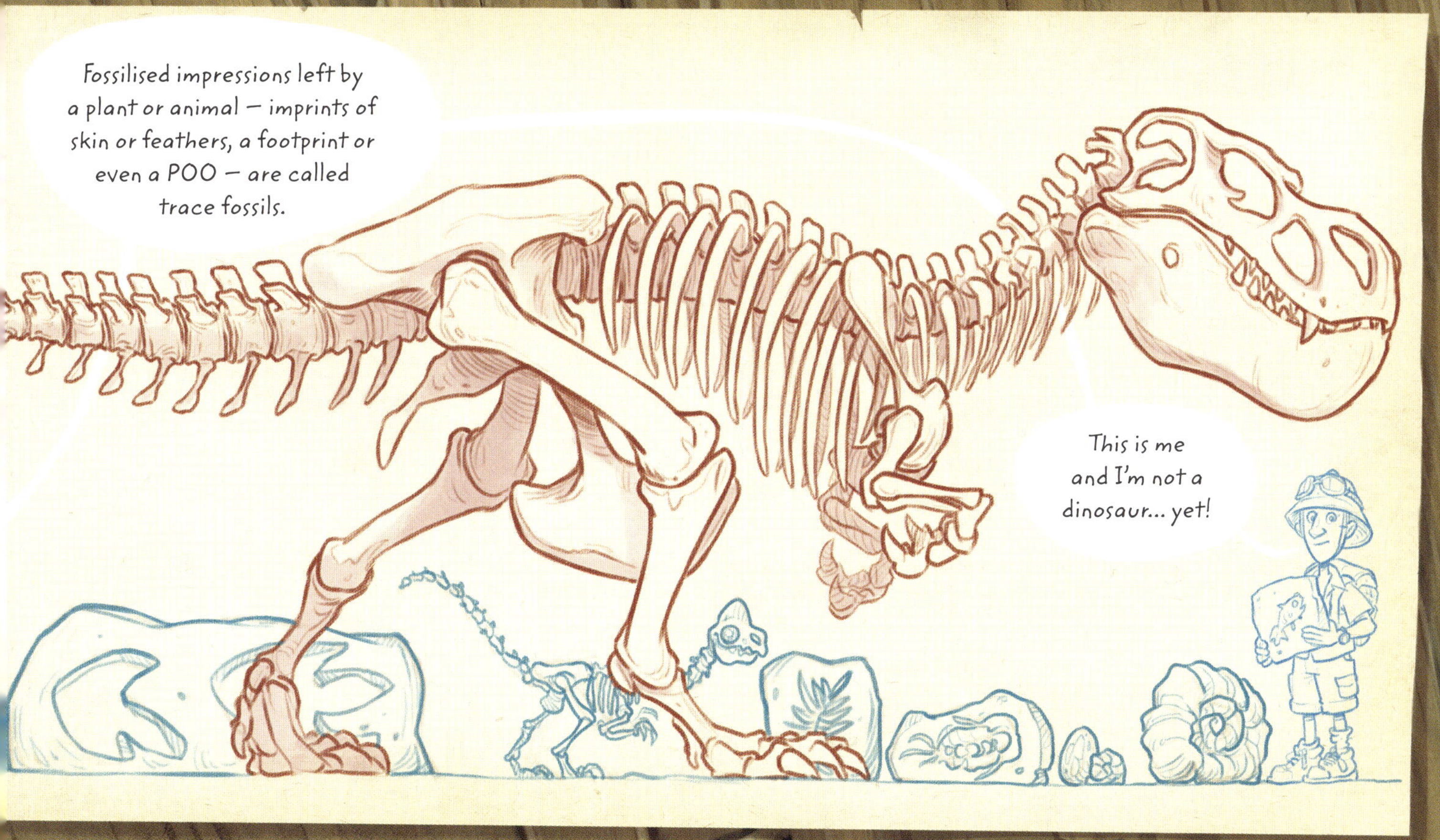

Fossilised impressions left by a plant or animal — imprints of skin or feathers, a footprint or even a POO — are called trace fossils.

This is me and I'm not a dinosaur... yet!

Water seeps into the bones sandwiched between layers of rock, very slowly turning them into stone as the water leaves behind minerals. This can take millions of years, but gradually the bones become fossils.

Millions of years after the Diplodocus died, rocks get worn away by weather or the earth shifts about. Someone spots a fossilised bone poking above ground. Hopefully, they call a palaeontologist, who (very carefully) digs it up.

The seaside is a good place to find fossils. Our coastline changes all the time, revealing new fossils. Next time you go to the beach, keep an eye out. You might be lucky and find one of your own!

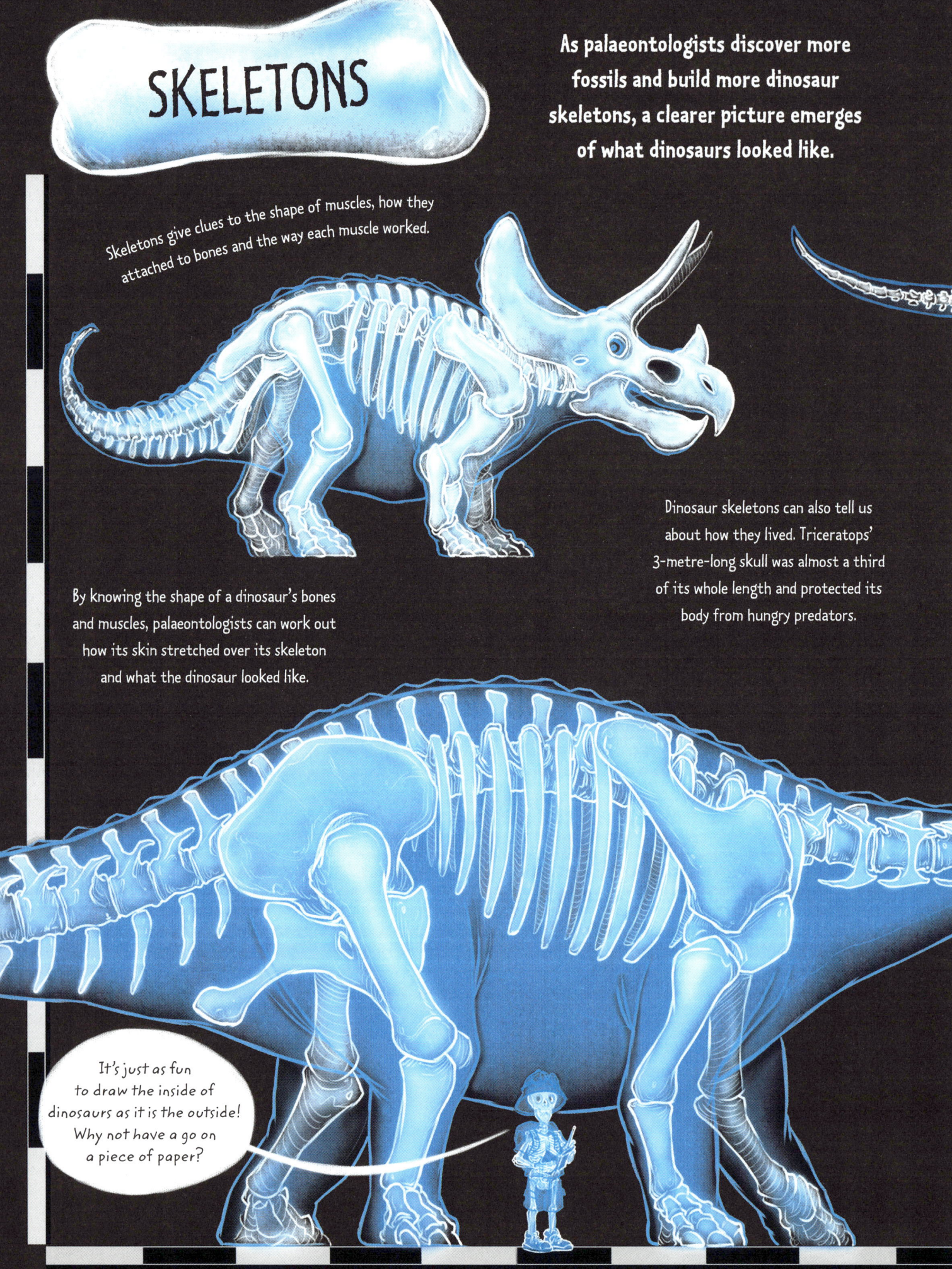

It's rare to find a complete dinosaur skeleton. Museums often assemble them by using bones from a few dinosaurs of the same type. Prehistoric flood waters may have separated the bones, or a hungry predator might've stolen bones for a tasty snack!

In 2023, a Tyrannosaurus rex skeleton sold for $5 million US dollars, but it was actually made up from three different T-rex skeletons. Only half the skeleton was fossilised bone, with the rest made up of plaster casts of other T-rex bones.

One of the most famous dinosaur skeletons, Dippy the Diplodocus, is actually a replica. The bones were cast from a skeleton found in America in 1899. There are 10 replicas of the original Diplodocus skeleton all around the world.

New technology can help us understand dinosaur skeletons. The Natural History Museum in London has an almost complete Stegosaurus skeleton. By taking thousands of photographs of more than 300 bones, they built a 3D computer model. This revealed its shape, weight and how Stegosaurus might have moved.

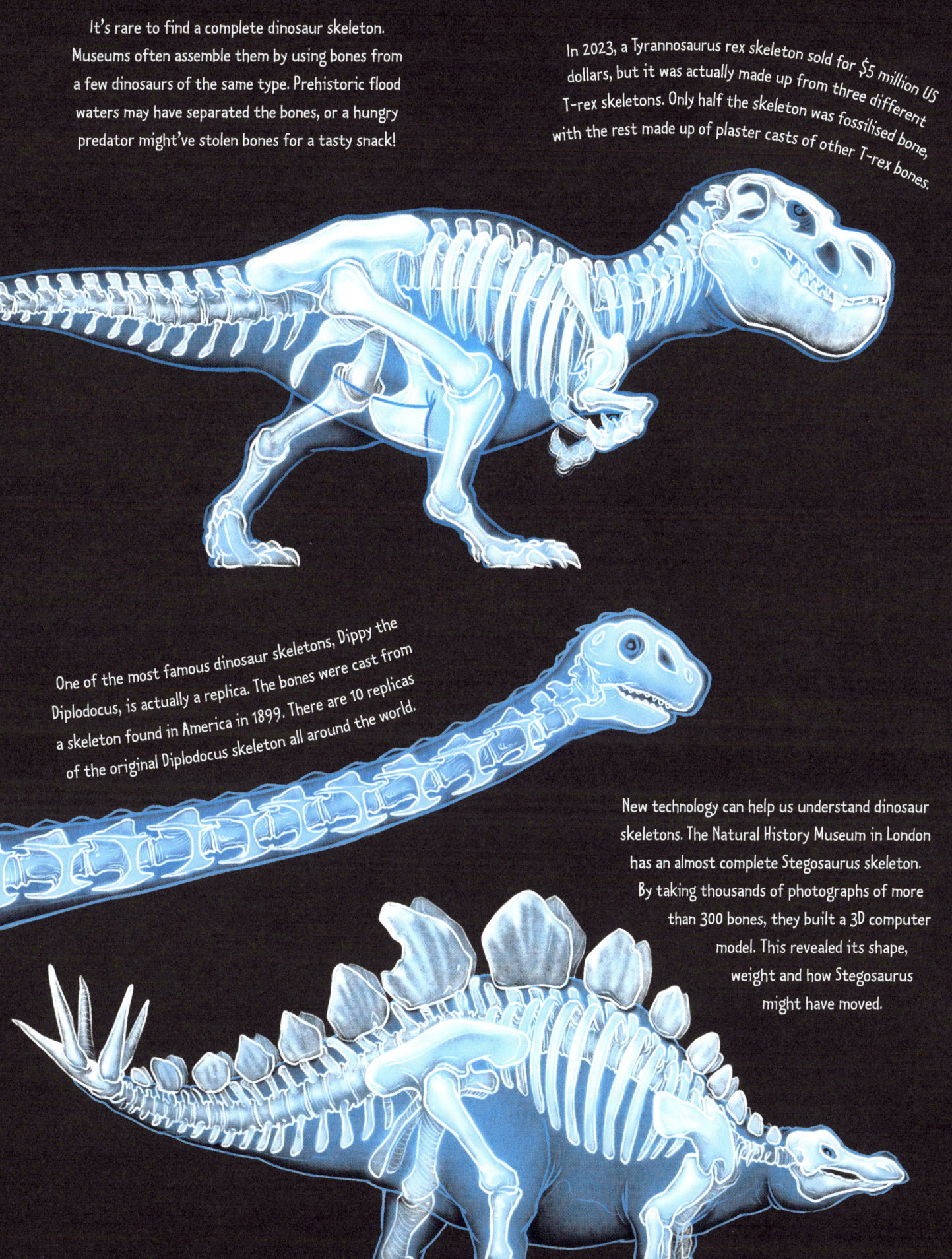

SAUROPODS

Sauropods were the largest animals EVER to have walked the earth! While palaeontologists might disagree about how big specific sauropods really were, we CAN be sure that titanosaurs like Argentinosaurus, Patagotitan and Dreadnoughtus were absolutely GIGANTIC. At around 60 tonnes, a Dreadnoughtus weighed more than 12 elephants. These plant-eating beasts had incredibly strong legs, long tails and towering necks with tiny heads.

The largest dinosaur femur (thigh bone) ever found belonged to the Patagotitan, an enormous titanosaur from South America. It was discovered by a farmer looking for his lost sheep, and was 2.4 metres tall. That's much taller than me!

If you're wondering how a sauropod could hold such a long and heavy neck in the air, their neck bones were full of holes, like honeycomb, which helped keep them light but strong.

Camarasaurus was a medium-sized sauropod with a shorter neck, and is the most common sauropod fossil found in North America. It had a blunt nose and an arched skull that gave it a very square head, with 19-centimetre-long teeth shaped like chisels, for eating tough plants.

CAMARASAURUS

If you could name a sauropod, what would you call it?

~~MEGASAURUS~~

~~VERYBIGOSAURUS~~

A typical sauropod loved its greens, eating at least 45 kilograms of plants every single day. I reckon that's about 150 lettuces!

The heaviest **Argentinosaurus** may have weighed up to 100 tonnes, and reached 40 metres in length, from its nose to the tip of its tail!

ARGENTINOSAURUS

BRACHIOSAURUS

Brachiosaurus' forelimbs were taller than its hind legs, which gave it a steeper tummy than most sauropods and angled its neck high into the air. This must have been ideal for ripping leaves off the tallest trees.

Diplodocus was an extremely long dinosaur. Its tail made up almost half of its length – reaching 12 metres or more!

DIPLODOCUS

EUROPASAURUS

Europasaurus was a small sauropod that lived in the late Jurassic period. They were isolated from the rest of the dinosaur world on an island, which might be why they only weighed about 800 kilograms – a similar weight to a horse, but they were less fluffy and had a MUCH longer neck!

DOODLE A... DIPLODOCUS

1 Lightly draw an oval shape for the body. Add four thick legs with flat feet — the near-side legs should have chunky thighs, and the far-side legs are tucked behind.

Diplodocus' rear legs should be taller and thicker.

3 Draw an eye with a pupil, and a tiny nostril. Draw a line around the nose and mouth and along the underside of its body. Add wrinkles where the legs meet the body.

While its body may be ginormous, Diplodocus had a teeny, tiny brain. It only weighed about 100 grams, whereas a human brain weighs 1400 grams. My daughter says I have a very thick skull and a Diplodocus' brain. She's so mean!

Diplodocus had an incredible neck over 6 metres long! But it only had 15 stretched vertebrae (bones) in its neck. You have 7 vertebrae in your neck. Luckily, they're much flatter, otherwise your neck would be 3 metres long…

Diplodocus wasn't the biggest sauropod, but it was still a colossal creature that could stretch as long as 27 metres – longer than TWO double decker buses! Have a go at doodling one below.

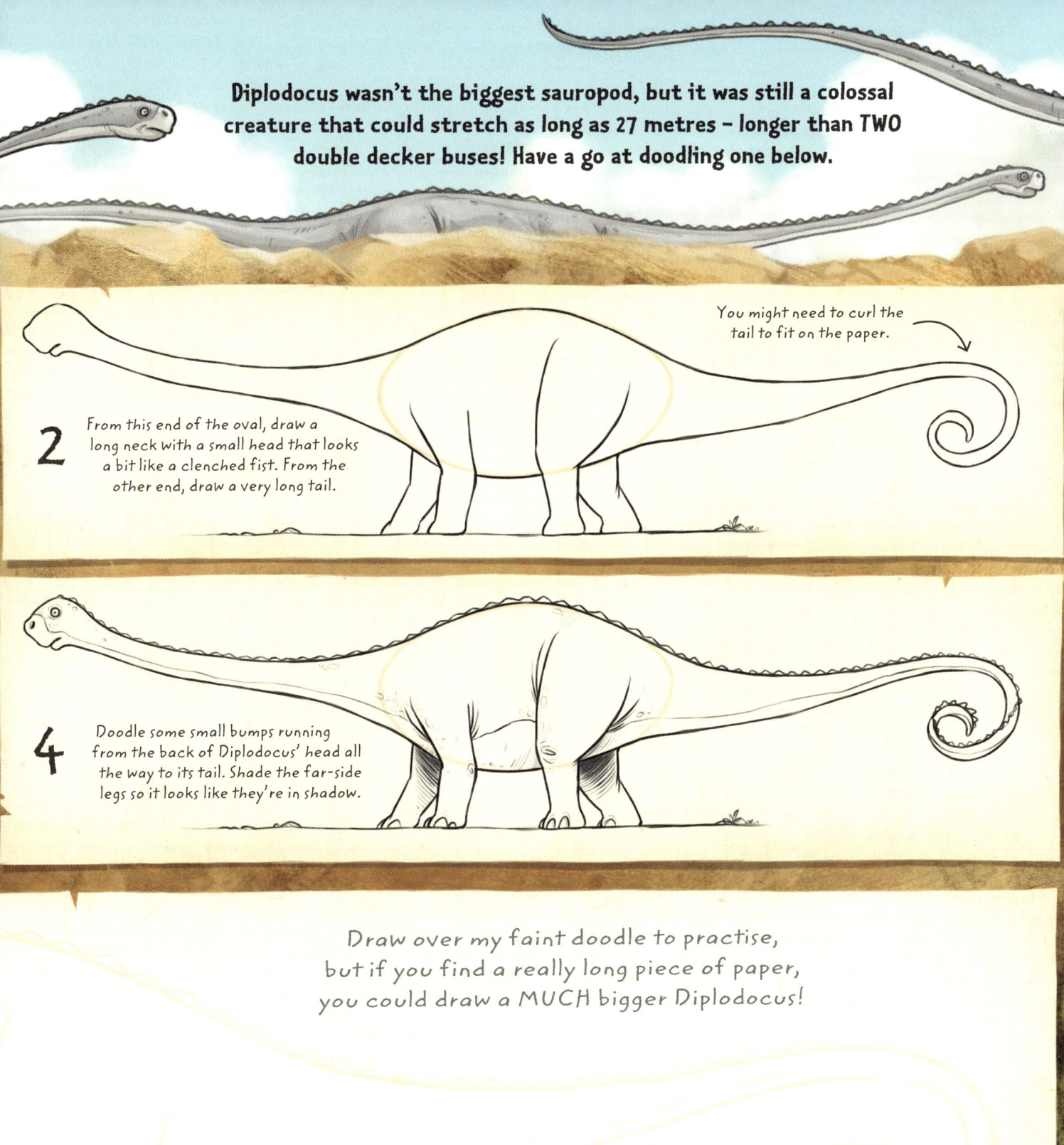

You might need to curl the tail to fit on the paper.

2 From this end of the oval, draw a long neck with a small head that looks a bit like a clenched fist. From the other end, draw a very long tail.

4 Doodle some small bumps running from the back of Diplodocus' head all the way to its tail. Shade the far-side legs so it looks like they're in shadow.

Draw over my faint doodle to practise, but if you find a really long piece of paper, you could draw a MUCH bigger Diplodocus!

Diplodocus had enormous leg muscles to heft about its enormous weight. A Diplodocus could weigh 30 tonnes (the same as 15 cars). Palaeontologists think it reared up on its hind legs to reach the highest plants, so it needed VERY strong legs indeed!

HOW TO DOODLE... TINY

Tiny is a young Diplodocus, who is actually quite big. He's probably the simplest to draw. Have a go!

1
Draw Tiny's head: a rounded square with a smiley mouth. In the top left, add an eye with a black dot in the middle.

2
Draw Tiny's other eye sticking out of the side of his head, and add a couple of nostrils at the top of his nose.

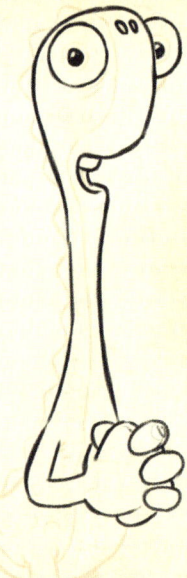
3
Draw a long neck, getting wider at the body. Add a bent arm and Tiny's hands: an oval with three egg shapes on one side

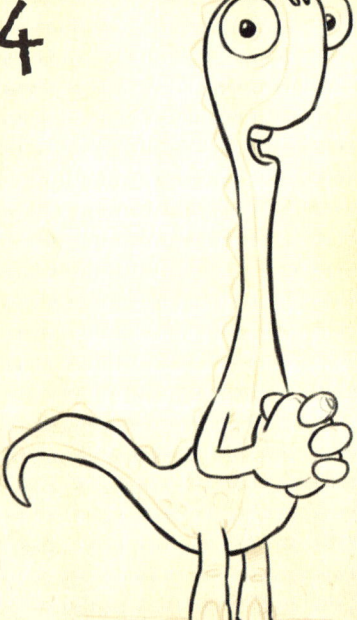
4
Draw the rest of Tiny's body: like a teardrop with a curved tail on the side. Add two legs with flat feet.

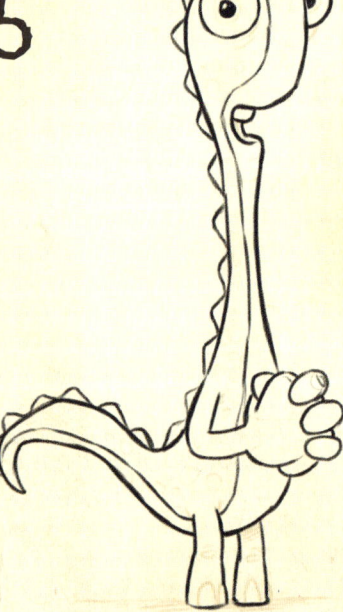
5
Draw a thin line between Tiny's eye and nostrils that follows his body, all the way to the tip of his tail. Add a row of bumps along his back.

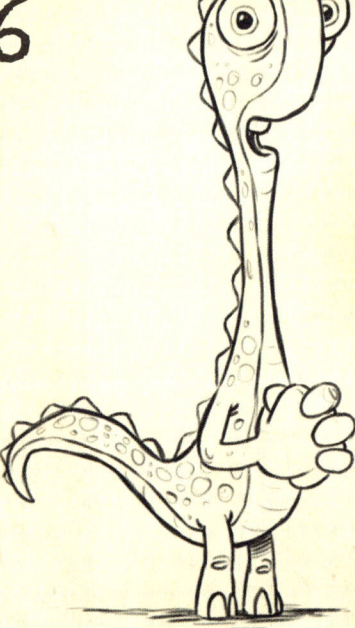
6
Doodle lots of details, wrinkles, scaly skin and some toenails. Shade the back leg, just below his tummy.

Add some colour if you like! Tiny is blue with a light brown nose and tummy and blue eyes.

You could practise over my faint doodle before you draw your own Tiny in the space below!

EGG-CELLENT EGGS

As far as we know, all dinosaurs laid eggs, just like most modern reptiles. Some dinosaurs may have looked after their young, while others may have left their babies to survive by themselves!

Well Done, Mum!

Maiasaura was a VERY good dinosaur mum — its name means 'good mother lizard'. Groups of Maiasaura made nests in the same place so they could share the task of protecting their eggs from predators. Once the eggs had hatched, the parents brought food to feed to their babies.

Dinosaurs that lived in hot places would sometimes scrape out a shallow nest from sand so their eggs could be warmed by the sun.

Dinosaurs that lived in cooler places often made nests in mounds of soil or covered their eggs with scraps of plants. As they rotted, the plants gave off heat. It was nifty and whiffy!

Home Sweet Egg

Each egg contained all the food a baby dino needed until it was big enough to hatch. Reptile eggs have shells that are bendy and leathery, unlike bird eggs, which have hard shells.

Maybe dinosaur eggs felt like a leather sofa? How strange...

Yolk

Albumen (egg white)

Dinosaur embryo

Amniotic sac (to protect the embryo)

Extra Large Eggs

The largest fossilised dinosaur eggs discovered were 45 centimetres long and had the same volume as more than 100 chicken eggs! They were found together, laid in a circle by a Gigantoraptor about 80 million years ago.

Many found dinosaur eggs have contained tiny baby skeletons — why not draw your idea of what a baby dino looked like here?

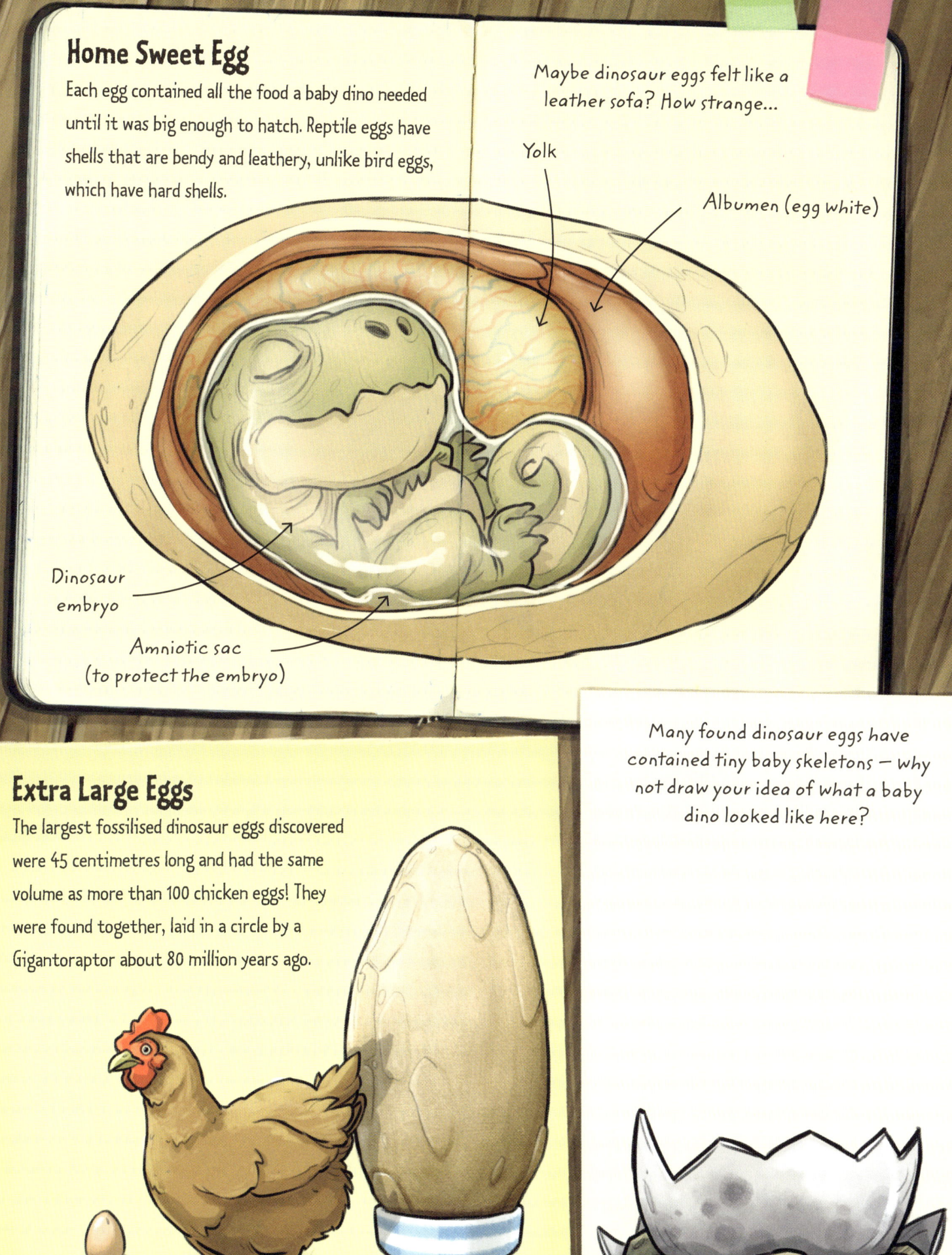

DOODLE A... PARASAUROLOPHUS

If you lived at the time of the dinosaurs, you'd probably hear a Parasaurolophus before you saw it. The long crest on top of its head was connected to its nose and was FULL of air, meaning Parasaurolophus could blow sound through it like a tremendous trumpet!

Parasaurolophus belonged to a group known as hadrosaurs, or duck-billed dinosaurs. A beak-shaped mouth is perfect for nibbling leaves – just ask a duck! Or Bill!

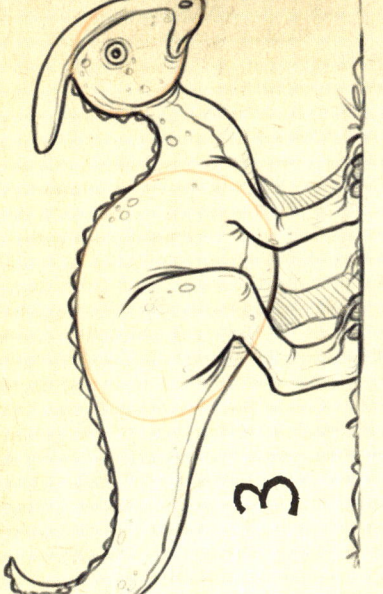
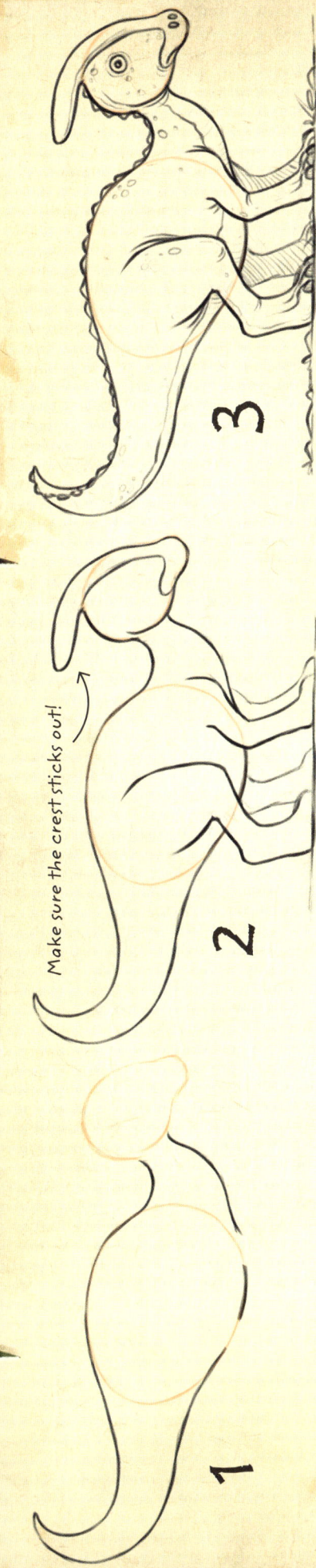

1 Start with an egg shape, but draw it leaning over with a very wide tail and a neck that bends upwards to the head.

2 The head is like another egg, with a beak and long, curved crest on one side. Draw the legs with bent knees and 'elbows', and long back feet.

Make sure the crest sticks out!

3 Draw a round eye and two nostrils on the face. Add bumps along its back, scales, wrinkles around the legs and pointy toenails.

This crest could be as much as 1 metre long – a big trumpet for a BIG noise!

Parasaurolophus bent their legs to scoop leaves and twigs from near the ground. Their powerful thighs also helped them sprint away from predators in a flash.

Use this faint drawing to practise a Parasaurolophus. You could even add some tasty leaves for it to munch on!

HOW TO DOODLE... BILL

Bill is a Parasaurolophus with a beaked nose and a trumpet crest on his head, which (I think) makes him lots of fun to draw!

1 Start with Bill's crest – a banana shape – with two round eyes either side, halfway down. Add the pupils, leaving a white dot in each.
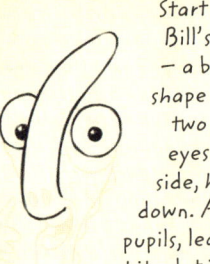

2 Draw a line from the left eye to Bill's crest, and a curved line under the right eye. Draw a circle around each pupil and add two nostrils.

3 At the bottom of the banana, draw a smiley mouth with top teeth. From the mouth, draw a long curvy line to form his body and a line from his right eye to form his neck.

4 Next, draw Bill's hand, with three sausage shapes for the fingers. Join the hand to the body with a bent arm and rounded elbow.

5 Draw a curved line to make a pointy tail. Add another line running from his mouth, following the shape of his tummy past his legs to the tip of his tail. Add two short legs with flat feet.

6 Draw Bill's other hand sticking out from his body, with three overlapping sausage shapes for fingers.
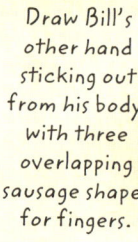

7 Doodle a big butterfly sitting on his fingers, and add a thumb. You could swap the butterfly for a flower or a bone, or a big stick if you like!

8 Now, the details: a row of bumps along his back, then finish Bill's smile with some bottom teeth and shade his mouth and far-side leg. Draw some toenails on his feet.
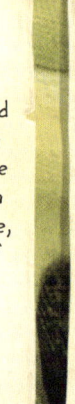

9 Finally, doodle wrinkles around his legs and knees, and on his knuckles, followed by lots of scaly skin!

Bill is pink, with a light brown belly and trumpet crest. He's got orange-brown eyes and purple bumps along his back.

Practise on my faint doodle before drawing your own Bill! Add sound effects from Bill's crest if you like!

DINO DINNERS

Dinosaurs were very hungry creatures who were always on the lookout for their next meal. They couldn't shop in a supermarket or walk to the fridge between sofa sessions, but they did have plenty of time to look for food. They had a lot less choice than you and I, but not all dinosaurs ate the same thing...

Herby Herbivores

Herbivores were dinosaurs who only ate plants. Some had long necks to reach the leaves of the tallest trees. Others had short legs and wide snouts to scoop up leaves and plants on the ground.

Prehistoric herbivores didn't eat vegetables like we do. They found their food in plants and trees – mostly tough, chewy leaves. In later periods, dinosaurs may have eaten berries that had started to grow as trees evolved.

Ginkgo trees were probably the first to offer a kind of fruit, but these may have smelled and tasted like vomit. Yuck! If there's not much choice, a berry-eating dino couldn't be fussy!

Fish

Dinosaur eggs
(I love a fried egg!)

Omni-yomni-yumni!

Omnivores were a type of dinosaur that ate both plants and animals. Some dinos liked to eat fish, insects and other dinosaurs' eggs. Raw, not fried!

← Insects

Crunching Carnivores

Carnivores ate meat, and LOTS of it! A Tyrannosaurus may have needed 200,000 calories per day, roughly the amount that 80 adult humans would eat today. Actually, a T-rex would need 140 kilograms of meat, equivalent to eating two adult humans every single day!

If you were a dinosaur, what would you eat? Doodle your ultimate prehistoric feast in the space below!

DOODLE AN... ANKYLOSAURUS

When you live in a world where giant predators roam, with teeth the size of bananas and razor-sharp claws, it's wise to be well protected. Meet Ankylosaurus – an armour-plated dinosaur. The head of this lumbering herbivore was covered in thick bone, while rock-hard skin and rows of spikes protected its body... But have you spotted its secret weapon?

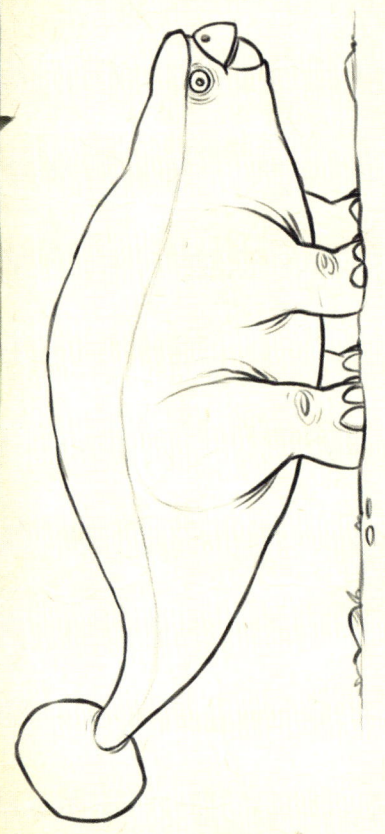

1 Lightly draw a long egg shape, then draw a long, low body around it with a round club tail on one end. Add four very chunky, short legs with flat feet. Opposite to the tail end, draw two lines for a stubby neck.

2 Draw two rounded triangles to form a beak-like mouth on Ankylosaurus' flat face. Add a small round eye. Draw a few rounded toenails and thick wrinkles on its knees, and where its legs meet the body.

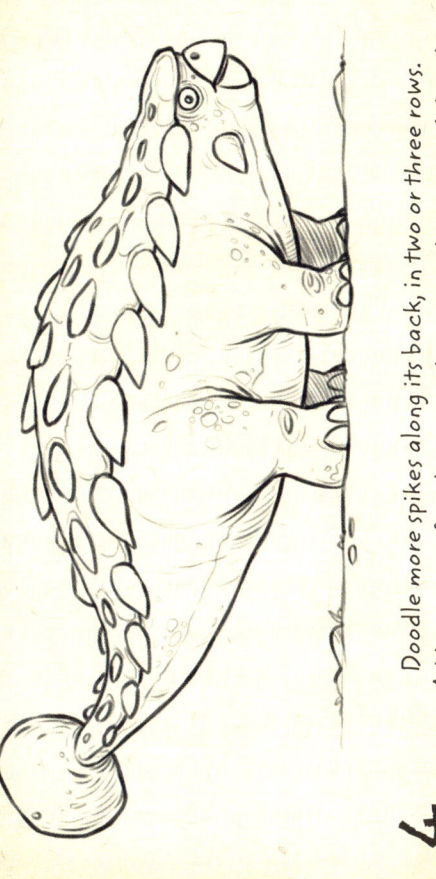

4
Doodle more spikes along its back, in two or three rows. Add patches of scales too and some shading on its club tail.

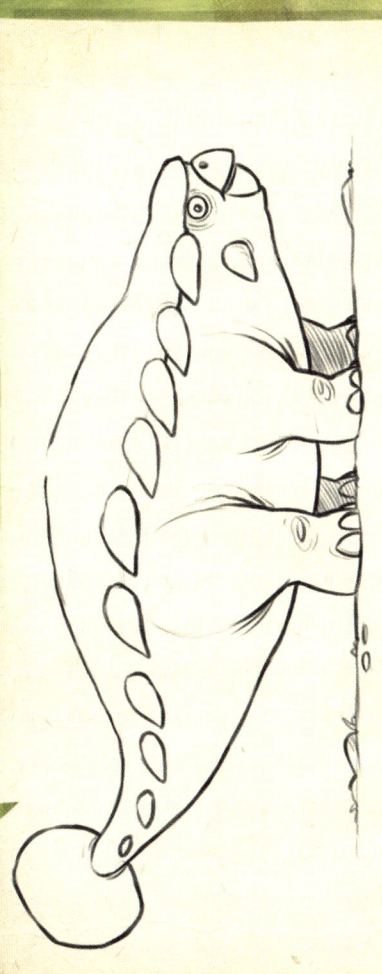

3
Draw a row of thick, pointed spikes along the length of the body, like pointy teardrops, and another spike on its cheek. Shade the legs on the far side of the body.

Have a practise go here before drawing your own sturdy, spiky Ankylosaurus!

Some species of Ankylosaurus had much longer spikes than this one. Perhaps you could try longer spikes on your doodle.

Ankylosaurus' secret weapon was its mighty club tail. One weighty wallop could smash a Tyrannosaurus' bones to smithereens!

Ankylosaurus was long, wide, slow and strong – like a living, breathing, prehistoric tank! It ate mostly ferns and other low-lying plants.

HOW TO DOODLE... BONEHEAD

Bonehead is an Ankylosaurus with a bony head and a club tail. Don't worry, he won't BASH you with it! Try doodling him below.

1
Draw two big, round eyes atop a flat nose. Under the nose, add a big curve for his mouth.

2
Add a couple of nostrils and three teeth. Draw two black pupils in the eyes with white dots.

3
Draw Bonehead's round tummy, stopping where his leg should be. Draw the top of his back and a bent arm.

4

Draw a hand with a couple of sausage fingers resting on his hip. Add the other arm with a curly thumb, and two legs.

5

Draw one finger poking up in the air and a couple of fingers to the side of it, finishing the right hand. To the body, add a tail with a flat end.

6

Draw a line from the corner of Bonehead's mouth, down his tummy to the end of his tail. Draw his club tail and add some toenails too.

7

It's time for details! Doodle two rows of small spikes on his tail, a tongue behind his teeth and some shading on his right leg and arm.

8

Draw the ground that Bonehead's standing on, and shade in his mouth.

9

Finish Bonehead with lots of scales!

Bonehead is orange, with a light brown tummy and a darker club tail and bumps along his back. He has orange eyes to match his skin.

Practise by tracing my faint drawing before doodling your own Bonehead below!

THE TAIL END

Dinosaurs are known for their whopping MEGA tails. Some tails were powerful defensive weapons and others helped balance the weight of their enormous bodies. Some tails even allowed dinosaurs to change direction in a flash while chasing their dinner. Eek! Let's have a look at a few...

Club Tail

Ankylosaurs (like Bonehead) are famous for their rows of horns, their bony back protection and also the hard, bony club at the end of their tails. They used them to clobber pesky predators. Even a hungry Tyrannosaurus rex might have had second thoughts!

What's a Thagomizer?!

Stegosaurus had a really unique tail, complete with a thagomizer – four long spikes, perfect for walloping attackers! The word 'thagomizer' was actually invented by cartoonist Gary Larson in 1982. It started as a joke, but it's now the official term used by palaeontologists!

Whip, Crack, Whack!

Diplodocus had a very long and VERY flexible tail, which may have been used like a giant whip. Using computer models, palaeontologists discovered that a Diplodocus could whip its tail tip at over 100 kilometres per hour, enough to make a T-rex wince!

Create your own dinosaur tail here. How long would it be? What shape would it be? Would it have spikes for protection?

Balancing Act

When I was young, T-rex was always shown walking very upright, with its head high in the air and its chunky tail dragging along the ground. By studying T-rex bones, palaeontologists are sure that their hips were tilted forwards, their heads held lower down and their tails raised in the air, which helped balance this ferocious dinosaur as it chased its prey.

I think I might topple over...

I'm in stealth mode!

THEROPODS

Racing across prehistoric plains on two feet gave theropods some handy skills – speed and agility! Theropods were a group of carnivorous dinosaurs that ranged in size, from giants like Spinosaurus to the tiny Microraptor. The oldest theropod fossils are 230 million years old and those predators probably survived on a diet of meat, but some later species ate fish and insects. A few may even have eaten plants as part of their diet!

Feathers Everywhere!

It turns out that not only birds had feathers, but probably all dinosaurs too! Lots of fossilised theropods have feathers on their bodies, and we can even tell the colours of those feathers from preserved pigment traces. Why do you think dinosaurs had colourful feathers?

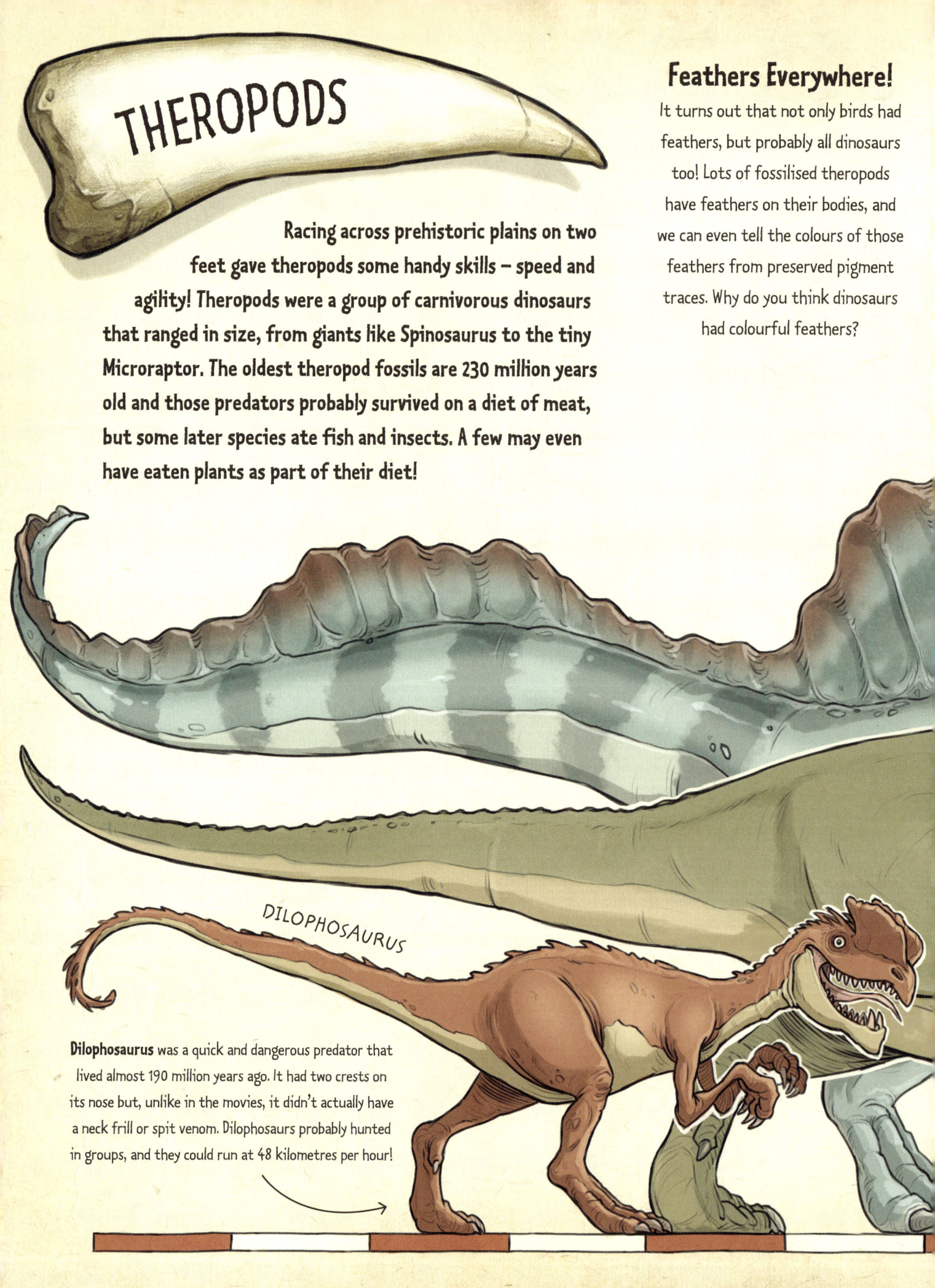

DILOPHOSAURUS

Dilophosaurus was a quick and dangerous predator that lived almost 190 million years ago. It had two crests on its nose but, unlike in the movies, it didn't actually have a neck frill or spit venom. Dilophosaurs probably hunted in groups, and they could run at 48 kilometres per hour!

Spinosaurus is the largest known carnivorous dinosaur. It lived in what is now North Africa and scientists think it spent a lot of time swimming in rivers and lakes, hunting fish and other creatures. Its wide, paddle-like tail may have helped it steer in the water, and the huge sail along its back may have acted like a dorsal fin, keeping it stable as it chased its prey.

Tyrannosaurus rex was a skilled hunter. It could run fast, had a great sense of smell, and had a bigger brain (for its size) than most other dinosaurs. A big brain meant it may have been smart enough to plan its attacks. I love dinosaurs, but I'm glad I don't have to worry about being stalked by a hungry T-rex when I'm walking my dog in the forest!

A **Velociraptor** was smaller than it is often portrayed in movies, only about 60 centimetres tall, but it was very quick, had a big brain and was probably feathered too. It DID have those scary curved claws on its feet, for slashing and holding prey still – ready to eat!

Eodromaeus is the oldest known theropod. Its name comes from the Greek words for 'early' and 'runner'. It lived 230 million years ago in Argentina and was minuscule compared to a T-rex.

SPINOSAURUS

TYRANNOSAURUS REX

VELOCIRAPTOR

EODROMAEUS

GIGANTOSAURUS

Did you know that Gigantosaurus wasn't a real dinosaur? When I was writing my picture book, I was supposed to write 'Giganotosaurus' – the real dinosaur – but I accidentally missed out the 'o'! But Gigantosaurus does look a LOT like a Giganotosaurus, a giant meat-eater of the prehistoric world.

Giganotosaurus lived about 30 million years before T-rex, and thousands of kilometres away, so thankfully these two fierce dinosaurs never fought over a meal.

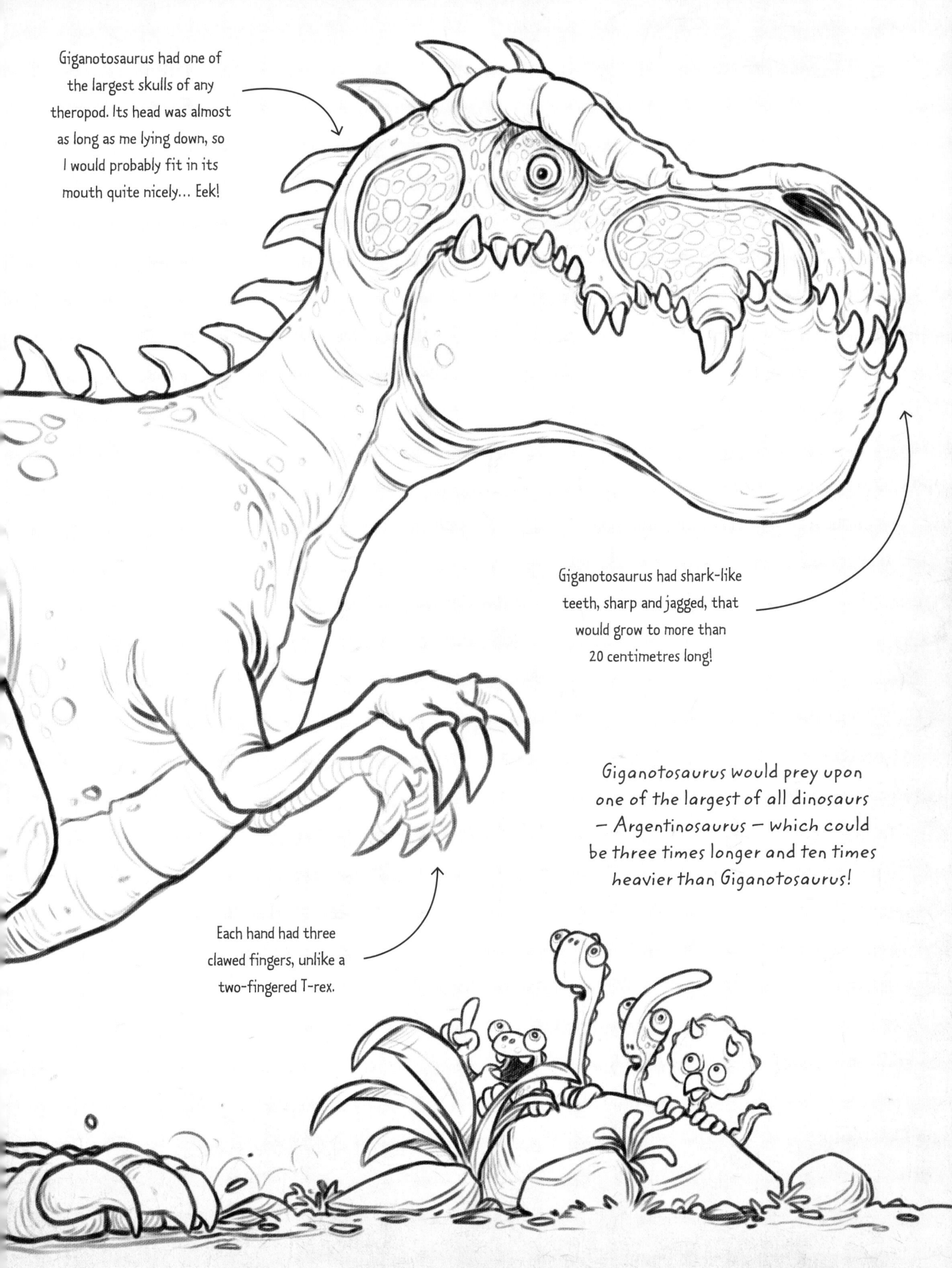

Giganotosaurus had one of the largest skulls of any theropod. Its head was almost as long as me lying down, so I would probably fit in its mouth quite nicely... Eek!

Giganotosaurus had shark-like teeth, sharp and jagged, that would grow to more than 20 centimetres long!

Giganotosaurus would prey upon one of the largest of all dinosaurs — Argentinosaurus — which could be three times longer and ten times heavier than Giganotosaurus!

Each hand had three clawed fingers, unlike a two-fingered T-rex.

HOW TO DOODLE... GIGANTOSAURUS

1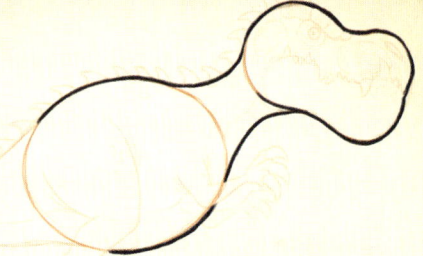

Gigantosaurus' body is an egg shape, with a head like a peanut. Draw those shapes, joined by a curved neck. Leave gaps for the legs, arms and tail.

2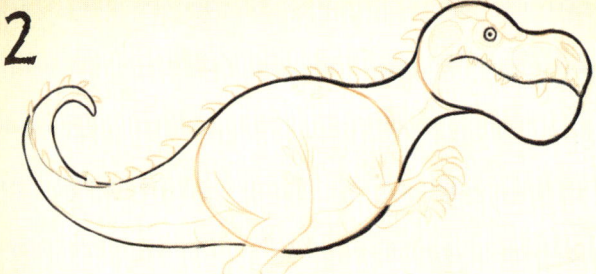

Draw a long tail with a pointy end. Add a wavy line for his mouth, and draw a circle for his eye, with a dot in the middle.

3

Draw lots of teeth, pointing up and down, a chunky eyebrow and a thin nostril. Add a row of spikes along his back, from his head to the end of his tail.

4

Next, draw Gigantosaurus' leg. Start with a chunky thigh, down to a long foot with pointy toenails. Draw his tiny arm, with three sharp claws.

5

Draw a line, from his mouth down his tummy and along his tail where his skin changes colour. Add the far-side leg and arm and shade them in.

6

Finally, add more details: hollows on his face, either side of his eye, scaly patches and wrinkles around his arms and legs.

When you've finished drawing all the lines, colour him in! Gigantosaurus has three main colours: green skin, a pale brown tummy and dark red spikes along his back.

If you want to draw Gigantosaurus even BIGGER, you could doodle on a BIG piece of paper instead.

TERRIBLE TEETH

Dinosaurs had awesome teeth. Plant-eaters needed strong teeth for ripping leaves from trees, and grinding tough plants and bark. The big meat-eaters needed massive teeth for killing their enormous prey. Thankfully, teeth tend to fossilise well, which means we can use them to learn more about prehistoric beasts, what they liked to eat and how they ate.

Sharp Bananas!

Carnivores had sharp, pointy teeth – perfect for biting and tearing into meaty flesh! What do bananas have to do with dinosaur teeth? Read below to find out!

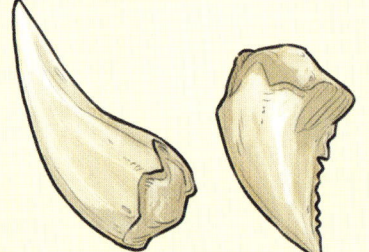

Some carnivores had dagger-like teeth, like a tiger's fangs (but bigger), while some were more like a shark's teeth, with their serrated edges. They had rows of these razor-sharp teeth, sometimes the size of bananas. Imagine the damage a mouthful of those could do!

Look at my AWESOME teeth! Can you imagine what I like to eat?

Slippery Snacks!

Fish and squid are slippery, so marine predators needed sharp, slender teeth to catch and tightly grip their prey. Spinosaurus had long jaws and narrow, smooth, sharp teeth, just like a crocodile.

Hedge Trimmers

Herbivores needed scissor-like teeth to snip at plants and large grinding teeth to turn them into a mushy pulp that was easier to digest.

Leaves and bark are very tough, so many plant-eating dinosaurs had strong, wide teeth to grind up their food before swallowing. The teeth of Pelorosaurus had sharp edges, slicing through plants like garden shears.

Diplodocus had peg-like teeth for pulling leaves from trees.

To help digest leaves, Diplodocus swallowed stones called gastroliths. They mixed with plants to form a mush in its stomach.

Some dinosaurs didn't have any teeth! Deinocheirus had a toothless, duck-shaped beak. It ate leaves and seeds, or used its spoon-shaped mouth and large tongue to scoop small creatures from the water.

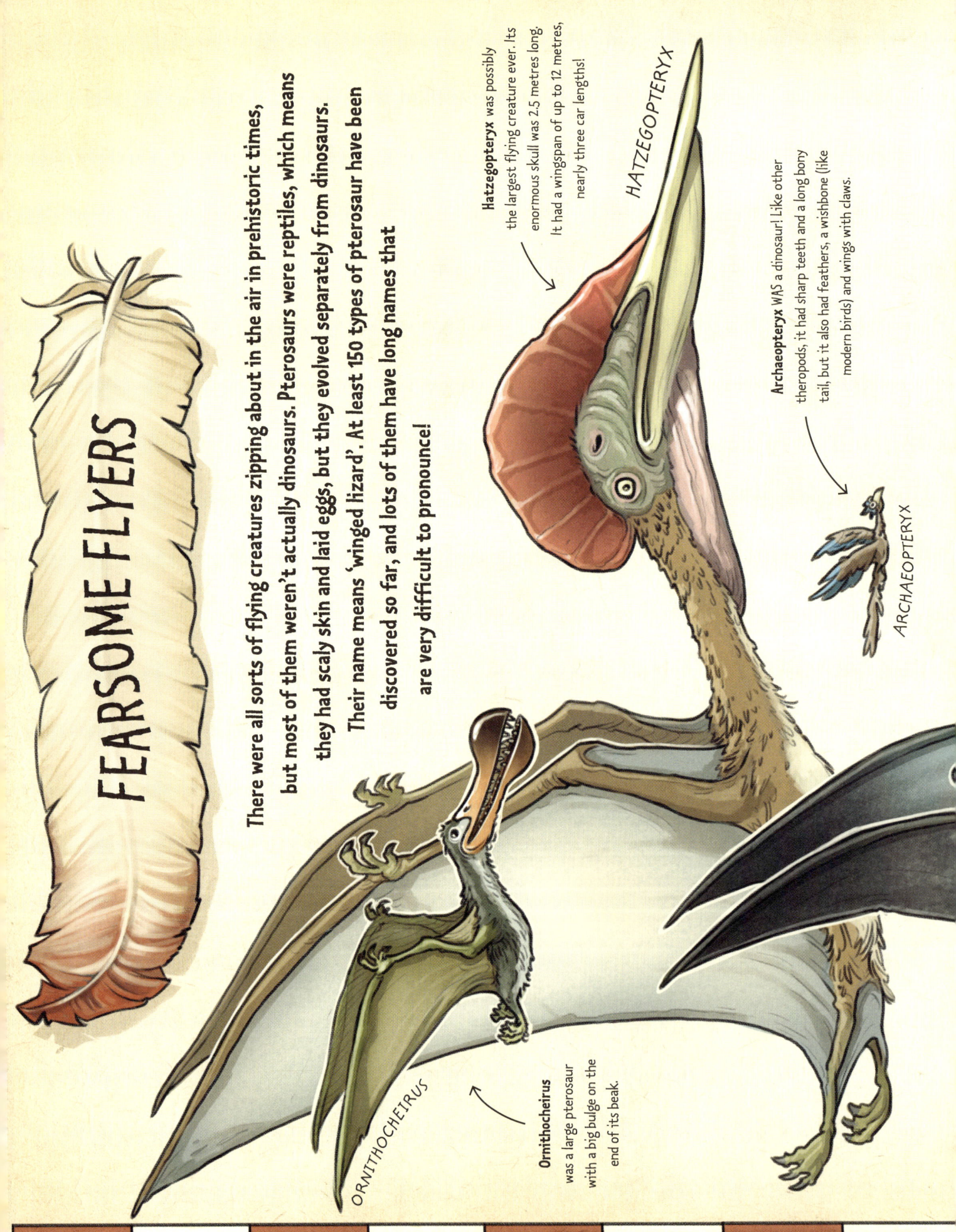

FEARSOME FLYERS

There were all sorts of flying creatures zipping about in the air in prehistoric times, but most of them weren't actually dinosaurs. Pterosaurs were reptiles, which means they had scaly skin and laid eggs, but they evolved separately from dinosaurs. Their name means 'winged lizard'. At least 150 types of pterosaur have been discovered so far, and lots of them have long names that are very difficult to pronounce!

Hatzegopteryx was possibly the largest flying creature ever. Its enormous skull was 2.5 metres long. It had a wingspan of up to 12 metres, nearly three car lengths!

HATZEGOPTERYX

Archaeopteryx WAS a dinosaur! Like other theropods, it had sharp teeth and a long bony tail, but it also had feathers, a wishbone (like modern birds) and wings with claws.

ARCHAEOPTERYX

Ornithocheirus was a large pterosaur with a big bulge on the end of its beak.

ORNITHOCHEIRUS

DOODLE A... PTEROSAUR

A pterosaur's wings had strong bones and muscles on the front edge, and some sharp claws, with a membrane of leathery skin forming the wing.

A pterosaur's bones were filled with tiny air pockets to keep them super-light, but strong, like a modern bird's bones.

Pterosaurs were superb flyers, but they could also walk around on land, using their claws and folded-up wings as front limbs.

Imagine looking up and seeing an enormous flying reptile, its huge wings spread so wide that they block out the sun and cast a huge shadow around you. What a terrifying sight!

1 Start by drawing the pterosaur's long beak, like a stretched-out pointy banana, and add one beady eye.

2 Draw the bottom beak and a crest pointing out of the back of its head. Lightly draw a long neck running into a teardrop-shaped body.

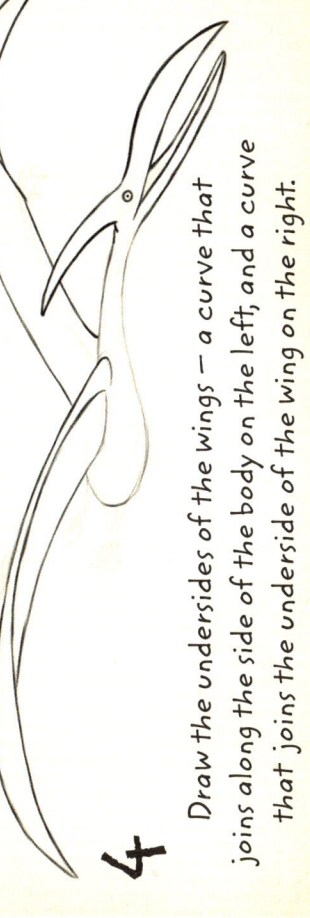

3 For the left wing, draw two lines like a blade of grass that's thinner in the middle. For the right wing, draw a shape like a curved, pointy paintbrush.

4 Draw the undersides of the wings — a curve that joins along the side of the body on the left, and a curve that joins the underside of the wing on the right.

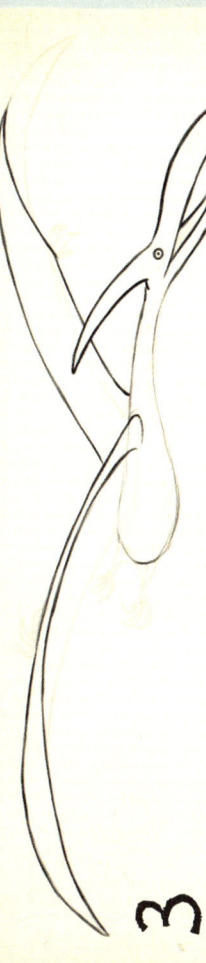

5 Add three sharp front claws halfway along each wing, and some tiny clawed feet trailing behind the body.

6 Add a few details. You can make your pterosaur fluffy or feathered, or a mix of both — it's up to you!

Practise drawing over my pterosaur. You could try drawing lots of them flying together with different colours and patterns on another piece of paper.

SERIOUS SWIMMERS

Prehistoric oceans teemed with life – this was, after all, where life began! There were giant reptiles, ferocious fish, snapping turtles and slippery squids, but you wouldn't want to paddle in the sea with this lot lurking beneath the waves…

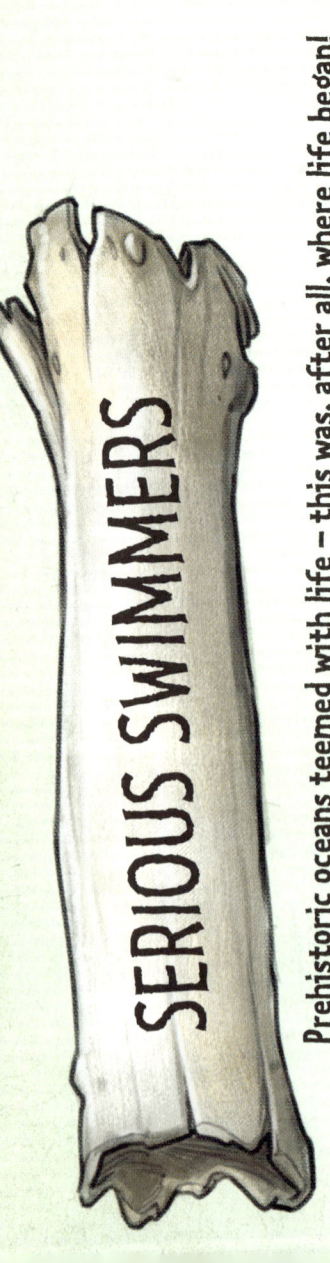

Coming face to face with a modern alligator would be scary, but meeting **Deinosuchus** would have terrified a dinosaur! This 10-metre-long reptile grabbed dinosaurs by the water's edge and dragged them underwater in its vice-like jaws.

DEINOSUCHUS

Archelon was the largest turtle to ever live. At more than 4 metres long, it was as big as a car! It ate a LOT of squid and jellyfish.

ARCHELON

Endoceras had the most fantastic shell. It was long and pointy and could grow beyond 9 metres! It looked like a stretched ice cream cone, but with a face and wriggly tentacles.

ENDOCERAS

Ammonites were huge molluscs that lived in a coiled shell. They are common fossils, and I found one on a trip to the beach. Keep an eye out when you go to the seaside!

AMMONITE

Elasmosaurus was a plesiosaur with a teeny, tiny head but a very impressive neck – a bit like an underwater Diplodocus. It was 14 metres long, but almost half of that was neck!

Dunkleosteus was a massive armoured fish. It could snap its jaws super quick and bite harder than any fish that has ever lived. It could easily crunch through Ammonite shells.

DUNKLEOSTEUS

DOODLE A... PLIOSAURUS

Pliosaurus was a lethal predator that grew up to 12 metres in length. It hunted large prey, such as long-necked plesiosaurs, ichthyosaurs and giant fish. Pliosaurus' deadly bite could deliver enough force to crush a car!

Four powerful flippers and a short, muscle-packed tail gave this reptile the strength and speed to catch large prey.

Pliosaurs were reptiles, not fish, so they breathed air. They returned to the surface of the sea to take a deep breath between dives.

Pliosaurus' skull could grow to 2 metres, most of which was rows of pointy teeth!

1 Around an elongated egg, draw a sleek body, with a long U-shaped mouth on the left and a short, curved tail on the right.

2 Add rows of long, pointy teeth, two oval eyes above its mouth and four leaf-shaped flippers.

3 Draw more teeth and shade inside the mouth. Add wrinkles around the flippers, a line along its tummy and a lumpy spine.

Draw over this faint doodle or on another piece of paper. Perhaps it could be chasing some fish, or even something bigger like a plesiosaur!

DINO DETAILS

Dinosaurs were impressive creatures, but they were even MORE impressive up close! While we can work out the shape of a dinosaur from its bones, it's harder to work out all the little details because fossils of skin and feathers and all the soft squidgy bits are harder to come by. But we do have clues...

Bumpy Skin

There are very few pieces of fossilised dinosaur skin, but there are trace fossils, where dinosaur skin has pressed into mud and left a pattern. These show us that dinosaurs had scaly skin.

Unique Physique

Ankylosaurus and Stegosaurus had tail weapons made from the same bony material called osteoderms, but they looked completely different. Ankylosaurus had protective bony plates that grew from within its skin, armour-plating its back. Stegosaurus' bony plates looked like fans, sticking out of its body. But were these for fending off foes or for keeping it cool in the hot Jurassic sun?

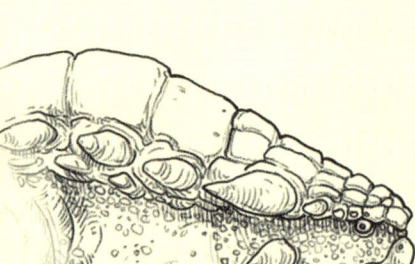

Watch the Horns!

Triceratops had lots of cousins with different horn arrays. Styracosaurus had six long pointy horns fanning from its neck frill. Regaliceratops' horns resembled a crown.

Competitive Crests

While Parasaurolophus had the loudest prehistoric crest, other dinosaurs such as Dilophosaurus and Corythosaurus also had interesting crests atop their heads!

DOODLE YOUR OWN DINO

If you've followed all my step-by-steps, you will have doodled a LOT of dinosaurs. Now it's time to design your own! You could re-draw a dinosaur from this book, or you could draw YOUR favourite dinosaur. A T-rex or a Spinosaurus perhaps? Maybe you prefer the herbivore Stegosaurus or an enormous Titanosaur, or a creature that lived in the sea.

Draw it here, or doodle on pieces of paper. You could draw a few, until you discover a dinosaur that you really like. Will it have horns? Feathers? Big eyes or little eyes? Pointy teeth? How long will its tail be, and will it have spikes on the end? It's up to you!

Now you know so much about dino features, you could completely make one up. Imagine a dinosaur yet to be discovered. Or you could mix up different dinosaurs, to create one that's so bonkers it could NEVER have existed.

This dino is called

....

Doodled by ....

STORY TIME

Have you ever wondered about the fascinating lives of dinosaurs? All the wild things that they got up to? It's like there's a story there…

My prehistoric tale, *Gigantosaurus*, grew from a Triceratops drawing, doodled in my sketchbook at the Natural History Museum. It got me thinking about dinosaurs, and I started to doodle some characters.

TINY

FIN

BONEHEAD

BILL

I found the old dinosaur books that I'd read as a child. Every now and then I doodled another dinosaur. I bought some more dinosaur books and found pictures of dinosaurs on the internet. But I hadn't thought of a story yet…

Stegosaurus

WHAT'S YOUR STORY?

Plot your story by doodling in these boxes. Think about how it starts, what will happen next and how your dino story ends.

You've designed a dinosaur, but what will YOUR dinosaur do all day? Will it make some friends? Save some friends? Or will it eat its friends? Yikes! Will it go on a prehistoric adventure? Maybe your dinosaur meets some of my dinosaurs: Bonehead, Tiny, Fin or Bill. What happens in YOUR story?

Your drawings could start off very small and sketchy. You could write some words if you like. Or your story could be completely wordless — some of my favourite books have no words at all!

THAT'S IT! FOR NOW...

Hoorah! You've made it to the end of my dino-doodling journal! Hopefully, you've drawn a LOT of dinosaurs and learned some new prehistoric facts. I've shown you how to draw some of my favourite dinosaurs in this book, including my friendly and fearsome Gigantosaurus characters, but you can use your new skills to draw the dinosaurs that YOU love. Perhaps you could start a dino-doodling journal of your own.

Your dinosaur-doodling journey never needs to end — mine definitely hasn't. There is still so much to learn about dinosaurs. Palaeontologists discover new dinosaurs every year and what we think are dinosaur 'facts' often change. We know a lot more about dinosaurs now than when I first read a dinosaur book, over forty years ago. Who knows what palaeontologists will discover in years to come...

Before you leave to continue your own doodling journey, I have a few bits of advice. Remember, drawing can be tricky (even for me) but it should be FUN. All you need is a pencil and a piece of paper. Draw for yourself, and don't worry about what other people think of your drawings. If a drawing goes a bit wrong, don't fret too much, just do another one!

KEEP DOODLING!

DINOSAUR EXPERT QUIZ

Are you ready to test your dinosaur knowledge? Answer all the questions below and tally up your score to find out just how much of a dinosaur expert you are. I hope you've been paying attention!

1) Which dinosaur character lived in the Jurassic period?
a. Fin
b. Bill
c. Tiny

2) What kind of food made up the diet of a carnivore?
a. Plants, like leaves and berries
b. Meat, like other dinosaurs
c. Both plants and meat

3) Which group of dinosaurs were the largest to ever roam the land?
a. Sauropods
b. Ankylosaurs
c. Theropods

4) Which fearsome flyer was actually a dinosaur?
a. Archaeopteryx
b. Pteranodon
c. Hatzegopteryx

5) What do scientists think dinosaur eggs felt like?
a. Smooth and soft
b. Rough and leathery
c. Slimy and gooey

6) Which of these dinosaur remains would be found in a trace fossil?
a. A dinosaur skull
b. A dinosaur footprint
c. A dinosaur tooth

7) Which real-life dinosaur was the character Gigantosaurus based on?
a. Giganotosaurus
b. Argentinosaurus
c. Titanosaurus

8) Which of these dinosaurs had a noisy, cool-looking crest?
a. Tyrannosaurus rex
b. Diplodocus
c. Parasaurolophus

9) Which brave dinosaur fought off predators with its bony club tail?
a. Oviraptor
b. Ichthyosaur
c. Ankylosaurus

ANSWERS: 1) c 2) b 3) a 4) a 5) b 6) b 7) a 8) c 9) c

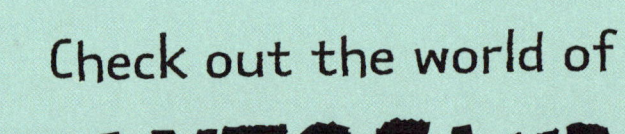

Check out the world of GIGANTOSAURUS!

The original story
Gigantosaurus (ISBN: 978-1-78370-051-6)

Puppet book
Gigantosaurus – Roar, Giganto, Roar! (ISBN: 978-1-80078-019-4)

Activity books
The Roarsome Colouring & Activity Book (ISBN: 978-1-78741-844-8)
The Ultimate Dinosaur Sticker Adventure (ISBN: 978-1-80078-644-8)
(New for July 2024) Where's Gigantosaurus? (ISBN: 978-1-80078-842-8)

Board books
Where's Giganto? (ISBN: 978-1-78741-823-3)
I Love Giganto! (ISBN: 978-1-80078-598-4)
Dino Egg Hunt (ISBN: 978-1-80078-296-9)
Santasaurus Surprise (ISBN: 978-1-80078-362-1)
The Scary Cave (ISBN: 978-1-78741-914-8)

TV tie-in books
The Story of Gigantosaurus (ISBN: 978-1-78741-569-0)
The Dino Sitters Club (ISBN: 978-1-80078-4482)
Crying Wolfasaurus (ISBN: 978-1-80078-233-4)
Finding Dinosia (ISBN: 978-1-80078-206-8)
A Light in the Storm (ISBN: 978-1-80078-207-5)
The Mysterious Maze (ISBN: 978-1-80078-506-9)
Giganto Games (ISBN: 978-1-80078-507-6)